THE CLOUD OF KNOWABLE THINGS

THE CLOUD OF KNOWABLE THINGS

POEMS BY ELAINE EQUI

COFFEE HOUSE PRESS

Minneapolis

Coffee House Press books are available to the trade through our primary distributor, Consortium Book Sales & Distribution, 1045 Westgate Drive, Saint Paul, MN 55114. For personal orders, catalogs, or other information, write to: Coffee House Press, 27 North Fourth Street, Suite 400, Minneapolis, MN 55401.

Coffee House Press is a nonprofit literary publishing house. Support from private foundations, corporate giving programs, government programs, and generous individuals help make the publication of our books possible. We gratefully acknowledge their support in detail on the last page of this book.

⌒⅄⌒

Some of these poems have appeared in: *Barrow Street, The Columbia Poetry Review, Conjunctions, Fence, Insurance, Jacket, Mississippi Review, New American Writing, Pressed Wafer, Shiny, Skanky Possum, The Spook, terra, Urbanus, 3rd bed,* and *Washington Square.*

"O Patriarchy" was included in *The Best American Poetry 2002,* edited by Robert Creeley and David Lehman.

"A Bend in the Light," "The Forest in Various States of Undress" and Round Corners" are from *Robert Zandvliet, The Varick Series,* Peter Blum Editions, New York, 2000.

Fourteen of these poems were also published as part of a chapbook, *Friendship With Things,* by The Figures Press, 1998.

⌒⅄⌒

Library of Congress Cataloging-in-Publication Data
Equi, Elaine.
The cloud of knowable things : poems / by Elaine Equi.
p. cm.
ISBN 1-56689-142-6 (alk. paper)
I. Title.
PS3555.Q5C58 2003
811'.54--dc21   2003041241

3 5 7 9 8 6 4 2
Printed in the United States

FOR JEROME

CONTENTS

⌒⁌⌒

Notes

NATIONAL POETRY MONTH

When a poem
speaks by itself,
it has a spark

and can be considered
part of a divine
conversation.

Sometimes the poem weaves
like a basket around
two loaves of yellow bread.

"Break off a piece
of this April with its
raisin nipples," it says.

"And chew them slowly
under your pillow.
You belong in bed with me."

On the other hand,
when a poem speaks
in the voice of a celebrity

it is called television
or a movie.
"There is nothing to see,"

says Robert De Niro,
though his poem bleeds
all along the edges

like a puddle
crudely outlined
with yellow tape

at the crime scene
of spring.
"It is an old poem," he adds.

"And besides,
I was very young
when I made it."

AUTOBIOGRAPHICAL POEM

The story of my skin
is long and involved.

While the story of my hair
is quite short.

In the story of my mouth
kisses linger over poppyseeds

and crumbs of lemon-scented cake.
There is a character who always builds

in the story of my bones
and a woman who refuses to leave

her gondola in the story of my blood.
But it is the heart's story

I most want to share
with you who also know this pleasure

of being shut inside
a vast dark place, alone—

as if at a small table
scribbling lies.

THE BANAL

Even with its shitload of artifacts, the everyday is radiant, while the banal is opaque and often obscure. I prefer the latter, with its murky agate, mushroom, ocher background music— its corridor of lurk. One hardly knows where one stands with/in the banal. Walls come together without a seam. Wherever we are, we feel we have always been. Poe, for all his special effects, is rather banal in his approach to the supernatural, i.e. overly familiar. Against the inarticulate velvet of this mood, one grasps at the everyday for relief. Thus any object can bring us back with the fast-acting power of aspirin. Any object shines.

THE SEVEN VEILS OF SPRING

1. ice water
2. egg yolk
3. pollen
4. cotton candy
5. fog
6. chablis
7. snot

NEGATIVE CAPABILITIES

I'm not a landscape
but if I were I'd be a prairie
with wildflowers embroidered
on the yoke of my rippling.

I'm not a child
but if I were I'd want to be
a teaspoon, an eyedropper,
or a chandelier when I grow up.

I'm not a novel
but if I were I'd be by Kawabata
or Tanizaki. No one can match
the elegance of their melancholy.

ASKING FOR A RAISE

Perhaps there is a color
I can sleep in
like a spare room.

Some uncharted green.

Some state I gladly travel to
in the center of a loud noise
where all is calm.

Snug in my cupcake hut
the difference between
sleeping with pills

and sleeping without them
is the difference between
talking into a telephone
and talking into a jewel.

Depression is an economic state.
Green is also the color of cash.

"All right, but what would you do
with more money if you had it?"

asks the businessman who greets me
with a lei of orchids.

"Shop for clothes," I answer.
"And treat my husband like a whore."

I INTERVIEW ELAINE EQUI ON THE FOUR ELEMENTS

Q: What is your favorite element?

A: Definitely air. It's the medium of thought.
Ethereal. Invisible. And even better than air,
I love heights. I'm the opposite of someone with
acrophobia. Space travel sounds appealing.

Q: Which element do you like least?

A: Water. It makes me nervous. You can't walk on it.
Both my parents are Pisces so perhaps that explains . . .
I'm a terrible swimmer.

Q: Being a Leo, do you feel at home with fire?

A: I like light, but not heat. I don't even like hot
sauce. I could never see myself as a pyromaniac.

Q: Which brings us to earth, what associations do you
have with it?

A: The earth has always supported me in all my
endeavors. I trust it.

OPAQUE SAINTS

We cannot see the fire within
that causes them to leap out of themselves
at inopportune moments

or stretch out on a bed of nails
with the blissful look of one
nursing on a lily.

So often, we too consider irrational acts
but wait holding our breath
until the moment passes.

Our boredom makes us happy then,
and Hell is the neat, well-organized place
from which we contemplate

the disruptive lives of saints
who break even natural laws.
Their faces are always luminous

and dry even when wet.
Their halos intrigue like jewelry
that can never be removed.

A QUIET POEM

My father screamed whenever the phone rang.

My aunt often screamed when she opened the door.

Out back, the willows caterwauled.

In the kitchen, the faucet screamed
a drop at a time.

At school, they called screaming "recess"
or sometimes "music."

Our neighbors' daughter had a scream
more melodious than my own.

At first, Col. Parker had to pay girls
to get them to scream for Elvis.

I didn't want to scream when I saw The Beatles,
but I did. After that, I screamed for even
mediocre bands.

Late in his career, John Lennon
got into Primal Scream.

Many people find it relaxing to scream.

Just as crawling precedes walking, so screaming
precedes speech.

The roller coaster is just one of many
scream-inducing devices.

The ambulance tries, in its clumsy way, to emulate
the human scream, which in turn tries to emulate nature.

Wind is often said to shriek, but Sylvia Plath
also speaks of "the parched scream of the sun."

Jim Morrison wanted to hear the scream of the
butterfly.

With ultra-sensitive equipment, scientists measure
the screams of plants they've tortured.

It's proven that if you scream at a person
for years, then suddenly stop, he will hear even
the tenderest words of love as violent curses.

And to anyone who speaks above a whisper, he will say:
"Don't you dare. Don't you dare raise your voice to me."

CAROL FEARED HER NARCISSISM

She looked hard into the void, its maze without walls, and spoke seven words into it. *Mercantile, narcolepsy, snow-blind, logjam, jawbone-of-an-ass* (which she counted as one), *tutti-frutti,* and *iota.* Briefly she toyed with the idea of adding an eighth word, *echo,* if for nothing else but special effect. Yet something held her back as if from throwing her very self into the pitch-dark air. She'd always suspected. Once out of her mouth, that *echo* would never return.

BARELY CONTAINED

I'm not sure
I want to.
My body wants to

see itself—
soft and shapeless,
plain as day

in the million mirrors
that pass
like thoughts

breathing
what is body
in and out,

its limits not
so obvious
as one thinks.

INVOKING MOTION

Monsieur Lartigue—
     Whether it was a wave or a runner,
or someone looking over their shoulder,
or even just a stripe, turning away,

you gave them momentum.
"Don't pause—move," you said to your subjects
and were able to see whatever it was
that carried them.

You, whose name rhymes with fatigue.
Give me that same jumpy elixir.

Action-hero: put me
in your antigravity garden.

       Rising, leaning, balancing, haunting
       (even your dead are animated).
       Thoughts are kites.

Muybridge broke it down, showed us the parts,
but you with a whoosh
push everything out of its frame.

Honk! Honk!

Get out of the way.
Nothing is still or separate.

THE SENSUOUS READER

1.

In autumn
take all the red and blue
out of a book.

Make wine
for winter's
sharp profile.

Then trace the profile
of other objects
with a knife

the way wind does.

2.

Open any book
and look to see

if the author
is inside the words
your eyes caress.

Read backwards
and up and down.

Skim diagonally

or just glance at some parts
and not others.

3.

Read by

        flowerlight

        petal-flashlight

or make a big
Pentecostal bouquet
of fiery words.

4.

The Silent Partner:

For one whole day
carry a book everywhere—

but never open it.

5.

Buy some expensive chocolate.

Then go to the library
and whisper an author's name
(preferably dead) aloud.

Wait for them to arrive
or for something else to happen.

Variation on the above:
Eat the chocolate and go home.

NOW THAT I KNOW
WHAT FEVERFEW LOOKS LIKE

What a disappointing book, and by a poet I like too. It's as if she had nothing to say, but still wanted to write and so names five or six different flowers in each poem thinking that will help. Or it seems like (at least there are hints that) something really big (and not, in fact, nothing) was going on in her life, only it was too chaotic to fit into a poem or series of poems, so she stuck with the flowers because she really wanted to write and have some measure of control over this big something or nothing (whichever it was) that she couldn't talk about, yet she didn't really want to talk about the flowers either, not with something else on her mind. And so the book ends up being of interest more for what it doesn't say yet seems to want to say rather than what it does say. And I guess I can understand that, having been there myself.

MANY UNHAPPY RETURNS

You can lead a tree to foliage,
but you can't make it think.

❖

Everyone needs a wise man
in a glass hut.

❖

Are we really as shallow
as our soap operas
are complex?

❖

I like most ideas
better than some people

and ideas I don't understand
better than those I do.

❖

18

Simplicity
underlies profusion.

Reaching the edge,
we begin again.

The severed head grows
obsessed with the body.

Dante put all the poets
except himself in hell.
That's why he's considered great.

ENTER HERE

Our maze will alter itself
to fit your specific needs
for delayed gratification.

Our movable free-floating walls
are happy to show the way.

Your eye likes being directed
away from history.

Memory is eating,
moving, buying
without a past.

Our maze is sleek
and self-correcting.

A new core (coeur)
that reorganizes
what it recognizes
in vibrant yet orderly ways.

COMING TRUE

Unlike water poured through a funnel
which begins as water and ends as water,
something said to "come true" begins as
something else. Then, slowly persists
like the stranger who keeps rambling across
your headlights or nibbling communion wafers
out in the yard. Though ominous at first,
he turns out to be someone who, in fact,
owes you money and has searched these many
years simply to find and pay you back.
So it would seem your life has not been
trying to kill you after all, and the air
you gulp is suddenly fruity Beaujolais and
the light slants in such a way to emphasize
not only the length and width of things
but also their marvelous depth.

THE OBJECTS IN CATALOGS

are made of light.
Well-lit or seemingly edible,
butterscotch and hazelnut light.
A bit vulgar, like starlets
the objects pose, pausing
as though in midsentence.
But really they are mute
—the story barely there.
Like children they wait to hear us
tell of the great Platonic love
we have for our many selves.
A vast literature reduced here
to a few short phrases: numbers,
letters, and of course, price.

THE OBJECTS IN JAPANESE NOVELS

Empty cages outline
the periphery of an unnamed thing.
Their emptiness shines
like lanterns on virgin snow.
A few flakes swirl up,
caught—as scenic views
are caught in parts of speech,
where wishes and schemes
grow gloomy as a shrine,
and hair is a kind of incense.
Here, even abundance is delicate
with a slender waist.
And sorrow, embarrassment, disgust
can be aestheticized too
if surrounded by the right things—
a refreshing breeze, a small drum.

THE OBJECTS IN FAIRY TALES

are always
the most important
characters.
Then as now,
the power to transform
is theirs—
the story
a way of talking through
(and to) us.
Shoes of Fortune,
Magic Beans,
are unlike objects
in magazines
for they awaken
us against our will
from the spell of abject
longing for more.
Only then do we live
happily ever after.

2.

They speak
but not
to everyone,

just those
ready to hear
and endure

what they have to say—

impossible tasks,

shine wrapped around
the seedvoice.

Golden apples
in the grasp of time.

"I'll climb up."

3.

(we are)
        Forever turning

things into thoughts

or caught midair
dangling between

the way children
steep their toys
in imagination.

A bird's heart
in him.

Clouds will catch
and carry him off.

4.

But finally, the objects
in fairy tales are words.

Beautiful as any object
we re-call

"water"
                    "daughter"

Grazing down
in the cellar
through the window
to the face,

then the tall man
made a ring of himself,

flames
trembling like cold,

old skirt
            old stockings—

pride and arrogance.

"If you stretch yourself
you'll be there
in a couple of steps."

WITTGENSTEIN'S COLORS

Blond
Tamarind
Bacon
Fog

Burlap
Winter Grass
Semidark

Tarn
Goose
Nutmeg

Brown Light
Hot Blue

Lion's Mane
Liverspot
Birch

BECKETT'S OBJECTS

"no things
      but nameless things,

no names
      but thingless names"

Difficult to grasp.
Difficult to know the use of.

Makeshift. Abandoned.

THE BURDEN OF BAD OBJECTS

"Bad floor," says the fallen child.

"Bad cloud," says the parade.

Bad dog. Bad penny.
Bad chemistry between the actors in a flop.

When he called me a moron, I was wearing my blue
sweater. Now *it* is bad.

Carnations always make me think of funerals.

The mirror upstairs adds ten years easy.

It's been a bad day.

Bad is a question of agency.
Bad is a matter of control.

We've all stood before rows of identical products
sensing one of them is bad.

Unless it is found and thrown away,
one bad object can ruin a whole life.

He erased his mistake and replaced it with the
correct answer.

She tore up every photograph where she didn't look
good.

MY TASTE

I hate being frugal.
I hate being extravagant.
Instead I prefer buying
small, useless things.
Like a hand reaching
into another century.
Carefully, I sharpen
the beaks of my pencil-birds
and fill in the sky.
Often, I feel I must
"buy back" everything
in order to recreate
some original state.
But other times, I shop
to make the world
an emptier place—
less embarrassed by its riches,
more aware of my grace.

WHAT IS MUSIC?

A distant traveler
        in courtly garble,
        feather and snow.

I push a button
        and it appears—

slow-witted at first
but later quick, very quick.

Its appeal is universal,
        but I do not think
        I've ever heard music,

only noise,
        dirty and wholesome
        on silent bread.

EVERYWHERE TODAY
WE SEE A LACK OF COMMITMENT

Who was the original
actress—Joan Fontaine?
I got the feeling
she was a little more lost.
Like that scene where
she's looking down,
it seemed as if she
really might jump
or was thinking of jumping,
whereas this actress
just looked like:
"What do you mean JUMP?"

"YOUR PURPLE ARRIVES"

Purple flower.
          Purple heart.

Heap of sharp
and muddy edges.

Bruise or blossom?

Harp strings
trickle-down
realignment
of morning's slow . . .

bright bug
with a crumb of window
on its back.

O PATRIARCHY

Inaccessible
              and remote

behind the drawbridge
of the penis.

Who knows
how your contracts
sprang up

without a word,
natural as rain.

The institution
of you speaks
for all man kindly,

but if a woman
is offended,
she finds no one there
to blame.

THE KILLERS INSIDE ME

when they are off-duty
seem like anybody else
at a party or in a restaurant.

They could even be witty
or give good advice
on which shoes to buy,

i.e. open-toe gladiator sandals
work best for celestial power-walking.

Really, they are not bad
when not cruelly maiming.

From now on, I've adopted
a live-and-let-live policy
toward the killers inside me.

THE SENTENCE THAT SWALLOWED ITSELF

Murky day,
murky thoughts—

without definition
or clear-cut shadow.

The tail of a fish,
the wings of a bird,
and the head of a flower.

Off and on
the air conditioner
makes a strange noise

grinding these myths
ever smaller
into atoms.

NEW AGE DIARY

I wake to the sound of tuning forks realigning my chakras, then gulp a glass of oxygen with my vitamins before creating the job of my dreams using positive thoughts and written affirmations. Next, I do my yoga asanas while burning appropriately scented, mood-enhancing candles to the goddess, followed by meditation on Buddhist and Christian scripture which only leaves time for a brief word with my angels, just enough to touch base and review the day's plans, as I finish a quick breakfast of a few almonds and a small banana. Then it's off to the homeopath, and later the shrink who is right across the street from the health food store where I opt for the grilled vegetable sandwich, and finally get home around four, so that there's an hour to relax with a cup of chamomile tea and my horoscope, unless I'm particularly stressed, in which case I might buy some chocolate and get out the tarot cards as well.

SNAPSHOTS OF WATER

Once skinny as rain,

I cannot help
but think of you as round

as the pot
simmering
on the stove,

the cup
            the world.

Never still
"and blue as the heart itself"

you write lines
on the body
            that drip

into other lines
with curious clarity.

Each shower
a palimpsest

as daily
some news, some murder
clings

—washed away?—

or most likely
just written over
in your own language,

hisses and murmuring.

You, the first mirror.
You, the first photograph.

O seemingly invisible
toward which I point my lens.

WOMEN AND MAGIC

A woman
in a wavy room
changes into starlight

as silence lifts
its hat
          in passing

and this
we call occult.

EARLY INFLUENCE

My mother lives *between* other people's words.

On TV they say this.
In the newspaper that.

Even those closest to her, when they speak,
are like a landscape she moves through
half-listening, unimpressed.

Not that she's unfeeling or aloof,
only that she prefers colors, flavors, textures—
prefers to draw or paint, cook, sew.

She doesn't know how easily,
just by picking up a pen,
their words become *yours*.

She isn't interested in such a transfer.

I've always admired this imperiousness,
this resistance to the so-called power of words.

It is perhaps her most political act
and one I find useful to recall when writing.

KNOCK, KNOCK

Hey, Ganesha!

Where is
        my shout?

My flight
        of bringing?

I want something
solid enough
to open like a door.

FOUR CORNERS

Storm Windows

A veil
to cover the veil.

A threshold
before the threshold.

A cloud-bruise
pressed between
pages of glass.

Stumbling Block

Eternally
tripping over it.

We decorate.

We call it home.

Focus

Right brain
and left
on a double date.

❖

The breath
polishes
the lungs' shoes.

Everyone Wants To Be Her

With her
winged robot

and chalice
of limeade.

She's the imagination!

WHERE YOU BEEN?

Everything changes
when you appear.
Head, a grand opening
that throws my idea
of far and near
out the window
where close is
close enough to smell
the fresh-baked bread
of clouds. And flesh
hitches its ukulele
to a star.
Like an entourage
you always did bring
your own horizon
with you.

FURNITURE FANTASY

Homeless club kids
living on rice, beans,
and Gitanes.

All day he forces them
to strip
           paint,

sand hutches,
and stain armoires
to the music of Billie Holiday.

Outdoors, under a tarp,
even in rain.
All this they gladly do
without complaint

for how else
will the owner
know whose love
of antiques is true

and who's a fake—

which urchin
to take
to his ancient
mahogany sleigh bed

and which to make
curl up in
the Morris chair.

TAKE-OUT FANTASY

He left a rodeo
to answer the phone.

Merely an expediter:
laconic tumbleweed
in the kitchen of desire.

He rolls the same phrases
over and over.

"Where to?"
"What'll you have?"
"You got it."

So picture him
in a leather jacket
over sweat-soaked skin,

his fly open—
his voice rubbing in
the extra hot sauce.

"Two onion rings, one
guacamole, one diet coke.
What else?"

Never angry or judgmental.
Never elsewhere.

To the almost unbearable
question of "what do you want?"

he brings utter simplicity—
                    efficiency.

Calm as someone
high in the mountains,
he speaks reassuringly:

"Fifteen minutes."
"You got it."
"Buh-bye."

ALIEN FANTASY

I wouldn't mind being naked
in their pupil-less eyes.

Just think of them coming all that way
for nothing but a closer look

as if Earth were one big peep show
advertising LIVE FLESH, LIVE FLESH

in undulating neon telepathy.
Who could be as fascinated

by our sloppy existence?
Who could care less about what is art

as they mix semen and stardust
or goose our boredom with joyride's probe.

And busy as we are, how else to justify
leaving work except in a crazy abduction

scenario? You check your schedule
again and again. Lost forever—

those four hours—like ancient teenagers
wander in some glittering arcade.

OUT OF THE CLOUD CHAMBER

and into the street.

Out of the art-deco prison
and into the cozy burning house,
the bleak house,
        the decadent steak house.

Out of the mouths of tulips and slaves.

Out of the frying pan and into the choir.

Out of mimesis endlessly mocking.

Out like a debutante,
        in like a thief.

Out of pocket,
        out of reach.

Out of time
        and into being.

Out of sight
        and into seeing.

Out of your mind
        and into your pants.

Out like a light
        and in like a lamp.

FURTHER ADVENTURES

The bird carries her off in its beak
her prettiness
     (ribbon   heart's rouge)
straining against flight, doing what she never
dreamed (actually, what she often dreamed
but never dared).   Up high
one can see the breath of Time,
its cold exhale. Time has carried her off
and the world is rearing up on hind legs
like the statue of a general on his horse.
The girl carries the world off
     (its prettiness and twin ugliness)
as surely as she is carried, yet can't stop
feeling she has forgotten something:
a necklace of beads, a train of thought,
a funeral procession with a broken clasp.
Something shining *beneath* the world
     (a word   a charm).
Something is calling her back.

LEAN-TO

The eye of the walking stick opened,
polished with ego (of good quality).
A crutch is a useful thing.

Shadow in shadow,
    character in character,
                mano a mano,
we walked the length of the city
(a wheezing   a many-chimneyed thing).

What is a story, I asked.
A story is a poultice, you said
applying its pressure.
A story is a blindfold
for leading the blind.

The ego glittered,
    the city slowed.
Cautiously, the eye
of the walking stick opened.

UNAPPROACHABLE AS EVER

Once again
you hang

like a snow
or raindrop

crisp in
your linen shirt

radiant
down to

the tiny creases
around your eyes

as you turn
your attention

toward someone else.

THE MOVIE VERSION

I am reading Emily Dickinson
when suddenly her poem begins speaking
in the voice of Mia Farrow—a young Mia
as she was in *Rosemary's Baby*

recites: "Heart! We will forget him!
You and I—tonight!" with resolution
in her strange faux English accent
as if she were speaking about Frank Sinatra.

And later I hear Haley Mills and Grace Kelly
try on the same line but with less conviction
so ultimately, it is Mia Farrow who stars
in my movie version, with her long hair

dyed blue-black and later crew-cut.
Mia Farrow who stands at the top of a stair
clutching a knife. "You may forget the warmth
he gave—I will forget the light!"

Mia Farrow in Victorian nightgown. Mia Farrow
in a poorboy and skirt, walks by herself,
visiting each word slowly as if it were a grave
on which she places the next word.

"When you have done pray tell me
That I may straight begin!"
Mia Farrow hails a cab. "Haste! lest while
you're lagging I remember him!"

ROCOCO

Come out from under
your plastic rosebush
and smell the linoleum.

A rustic and her swain
observe the chess game
of others more witty

and pretty
and comfortable
in society.

O there is always a fly
in the petitfours.
A beggar in the richest dream.

THE LOST POEMS

Your Average Dream
Fetish-Shroud
Victor Mature's Kiss
The Snow Queen's Summer House

In a Nutshell
De-composing
Vintage Blouse
Politics and Vaseline

Mister Preface
Charm-Quake
Postponing the Future
Notice Each Part

The Cloud's Tantrum
Harlequin with a Gun

A BEND IN THE LIGHT

A bend in the light.
A dross in the drift.
A tilt in the storm.
A gleam in the ditch.

A grace in the gloom.
A kink in the sand.
A spring in the fire.
A lilt in the hand.

A snare in the common.
A hare in the shed.
A mesh in the fury.
A glare in the blurring.

A stretch in the arc.
A pulse in the bark.
A fork in the wave.
A heft in the sway.

THE FOREST
IN VARIOUS STATES OF UNDRESS

Tying
     and untying.

Desire
     and revulsion.

Aren't you tired of this game
said the branch
to whatever would listen.

No, no, said the robin.
Too pretty from afar.

Too pretty up close, said the ant
in its microscopic spotlight.

Only the present leaves us cold.
Sits and does nothing
with its grim jack-o-lantern grin.

INTERSECTIONS

I'm at the corner of Can't & Won't.
In the kiosk between Aroma & Automatic,

Squirm & Squall,
Minimal Art & Minimum Wage.

I'm trying to get to Hilt & Vine.
The high-priestess in the high-rise

and the persona in the persona-non-grata dept.
both told me that if I cut across Performance

& Fugue, Mayday & Kind, it would put me
on the quad next to the grid

near Bittersweet & Icarus
and from there I could walk.

ROUND CORNERS

Soft as
the road's
shoulder.

Map seen through
the spyglass
of touch.

Cross-hatched
pelt of rain.
Its mouse-bite
in winter.

A SENTIMENTAL SONG

We feel more than see
the stars white as radishes
and as sharp.

To we who always look down,
it's right that they be *in* the ground.
We love winter because it makes inner

seem even more inner
                    and crackling.

✣

Cold is a fragrance
that clings to the skin
and smells cold.

Imagine a perfume called "Snow"
and another called "Drizzle"
and another called "January"

and all of them—free.

✣

Just for today, I'd like to
step into someone else's list.
Run their errands. Wish their wish.

Today is St. Ita's day (the most famous
woman saint in Ireland after Brigid).
She is said to have reattached

the head to the body
of a man who'd been beheaded
and to live only on food from heaven.

Meanwhile the weather here is gray
but optimistic, aspiring to (I'm not sure what).
The slant of something moving up and away.

TRENTON LOCAL

for Susan Wheeler

Crows ride slow
rafts of ice downstream:
Barge music

under sky's
low ceiling

Openings
open one after
another

Wreaths of space
crown weeds, thorns

You start in
the middle. You start
again here.

Factory
                    Reverie

Shadowplay
behind the scrim of
production

Crime, sex, art,
greed, and sports

One story
gets folded into
another

Even trees
play a part

Enhancing
the lullaby of
certain words

repeated
        precisely

O wall that
asks eternally
"SKEETER, WHY?"

I love your
lurid scrawl!

Yellow meets
and mingles with me
and dark red

Courthouse flag
waves good-bye

Cables sag
and stretch to meet their
connections

Spring is a
station too

She scribbles
on watery screens,
sheets of air . . .

feather-pen
        quarter notes

The jagged
lace of broken glass
unweaving

Billboards talk
vis-à-vis

So where is
this invisible
leading man?

scattered in
        time and place

Four brides left
forever in the
bridal shop

Ashes cloud milk.
Mist veils rocks.

Train's motion
makes the landscape seem
to tremble

A girl in
blue, smoking

Wedged in—this
time you start closer
to the end

Not wanting
to arrive

The hills of
empty packaging
dazzle us

A shrine to
appetite

We've consumed
all that and still are
ravenous.

Feeding our
frustration

"The best part
of my day would be
the bagel."

Sloppy and
    Mythical

A soft vague
border between speech
and silence

between the
wild and the tame

To dream of
a tunnel suggests
birth or death

Gravediggers
work in shades.

Is it jade
or black—the river's
lost mood ring?

Paper fish
scale the sky

Spare car parts
spread out like bones to
be sun-dried

Gears caught in
the crabgrass

What is elf
lubricant? And where
can I buy?

Winter's quick
cameo

A whistle
that never sounds the
same way twice

CAN'T COMPLAIN

We were just a sea of talking heads
getting carried away on a moving sidewalk
with space around the names
we kept dropping and picking up.

And though we thought it normal to think
one day the whole shebang would collapse,
our stories kept telling us elsewhere.
It was the anti-apocalypse and it wasn't

going to go away because we were bored.
Try thinking less of progress and more of others
is what it said. What's wrong with everyone
being rich? Oh nothing, nothing at all, we chimed

as we slipped past the scarlet beast at the door
with the sign that read: too much allegory
may be hazardous to your health. You see,
we were trying to return to an earlier motif

when "outside" was an aspiration in and of itself
and one could eat natural phenomena for breakfast
and live like a king cockroach on a cloud-stained
couch. All our rainy days saved up for this.

SOMEWHERE PAST CYBERSPACE

You won't find me.
Another galaxy
is where I'm headed.
A single mom in space
is what I'll be.
Giving birth—
being human,
what's it mean
so far from earth?
My baby's feet
won't touch the ground.
He'll float beside me
for light years.
Pioneers—evolving
a new relationship to property.
It's written here as prophesy.
A single mom in space is what I'll be.

PIVOTAL GAPS

Characters unhook us.
My habits get tried on
by the protagonist in the novel.
We trade places.
She likes seeing the future
and I like knowing
how the era ends after the book.
But we never quite see ourselves
at the same time. Her opera glasses
and silk-drenched movements
get detached and rewritten
in my anxious picking up and putting down
the rhythm of a whole summer
until finally, like Shiva,
she drinks the poison cup (unhappy ending)
out of compassion for me.
Perhaps you think she had no choice,
but I know differently.

A CUP OF JOE

glasses shine.   light wipes
the counter.   the room lets
anyone in.   mouth sips hand
as if drawing drink.   what
is it books say—"flooded
with warmth."   backlit. face
ajar. reading other people's
mysteries. cooler in the margins.
a splash of solitude ends here.

DESSERT

This caramel is scriptural.
This lemon tart more beautiful than a Matisse.
It's the way paintings (and heaven) taste
as they dissolve and we internalize them.

Gurus know it.
Don't you remember after they slapped us
with peacock-feather-fans,
the little piece of rock candy
we each got and sucked in the corner,
thinking that if the mantras didn't work,
at least there was this.

FOR AUGUST IN APRIL

Now that we are back
to the beginning
of the alphabet—

its green apron
              and aquarium days,

its archers who aim
              at nothing at all,

who prefer to let
the targets come to them.

Suddenly, we are ashamed
of trying to connect things
with artifice and would prefer
the actor speak his part
in a series of asides.

We aspire to an assortment.

The asylum shines
              with symptoms

that are, at first, at attention
then later, at ease

as if consciousness
were nothing but an auction house.

The radio is not on, yet
much is still audible—

              auguries, aubades.

73

RETURN OF THE SENSUOUS READER

Reading Nude vs. Reading Barefoot

Unless you are especially comfortable
with your body, reading in the nude is likely
to be more of a distraction than an enhancement.

A better compromise that still lends an air of ease
and intimacy is reading barefoot. Just imagine
walking barefoot over the words you're reading.
Note: this is especially pleasurable to do in public.

Turning Down the Sound

Remove all the words from a poem;
keep only the punctuation.

Can You Recognize This Famous Poem?

,

.

.

A sublime treat for purists
or good exercise to cleanse the palate.

The Text as Symptom

Read the same poem at different times
and record your response in terms of
purely physical sensations: heartbeat, pulse, etc.

Warning: hypochondriacs, don't get carried away
with this one.

Does It Make Any Difference?

Change the gender of all the pronouns in a poem
and see for yourself.

Against Memorization

Memorizing a poem is a good way to destroy it.
You think it will bring you closer (like getting
a tattoo) but the poem does not reside in its words
and that is all you'll be left with.

Never again will you encounter it by chance
in the casual cruising-space that spells romance.
Rereading works better.

All Books Are Oracles

Formulate your question.
Use the standard open-at-random-
and-point method.

Live according to the words.

AFTER AND IN KEEPING WITH H.D.

When I am a current
                lifted up—
can you hear eclipses' seasoning?

When you are a cure-all,
there is no signal,
                        nor sorcery
trailing along.

When I am a curve-ball
                made of shelter,
O can you hear distance receding?

When you are a comment,
there is no sour cherry
trudging across sanctuary gravel.

CAREER

In trees

the leaves have
finally found
their niche.

COURTESANS LOUNGING

One lights a candle.

One blows it out.

Revisiting old habits
should please use the servants' entrance

      (also known as the five senses)

and don't forget to wipe your feet.

RESET

Fingers
     and page

stained saffron
with first light.

Flight the swoop
of cars below, the war whoop
of birds casting spells.

The man of pipes
and the man of ladders
ascend, descend, then find a level.

Putting one's head in the clouds,
one realizes how stubborn they (clouds) are—
how long they take to move,

the way they insist,
with their many-colored inks,
on writing backwards

     ✤

Balcony

Three empty
beer bottles rest
side by side
in the nest
of a cinderblock

of tall wild grass.

Beside a ragged palm
a ratty rattan chair
leans forward.

Like an old couple
the white plastic chairs
are pushed close.
Their arms touch gently.

❖

Humming a nondescript incandescence,
the city runs itself without need of words.
I dreamt last night of a choice between two things

(A & B) but can't remember what they were
or which I decided on. One had certain features,
the other was just darkness.

Mornings are so dazzling, I hadn't noticed
this quality in them before and only wanted
to prolong night for as long as possible, forever.

It seems I've never carried anything this heavy
up a flight of stairs: worlds piggybacked
upon worlds. Every ocean a drop in the bucket.

But you didn't try to persuade me to put it down.
You said: "Look, what you carry is an image.
How much can an image possibly weigh?"

❖

Periodically,
Miro-like
blue stick-figures

walk across
the sky

like matches
waiting to be lit.

Connect
the turquoise dots.

Ash & Rain.

Decorators do different things
with rooftops.

One makes a Roman arch
complete with tendrils of grapes.

Another is simply
a stage set

for automatons'
pas de deux.

A little of this.
A little of postmodernist that.

❖

Dreamt I visited Mi Casa Roja.
Mi Casita Rojita.
My little pink cottage—

a Mexican restaurant
where they show videos
of my old poetry readings

but I can't get a table.
The waiters, the customers
everyone in my own cunt too busy to see me!

Finally, found a woman I knew and read
a passage aloud to her about candlelight.
"You know how I feel about candlelight."

Later, walked with swaying hips up stairs
followed by an anonymous, clove-scented man.
As in most movies, I never got to see what we did.

Mi Casa Roja: perhaps I will visit you again soon.

❖

    Last night, it wasn't dreams I remembered but
falling asleep and this morning—waking. The back
and forth of it, prolonging those two states so as
to be able to re-create them again.

    We are at war. How old-fashioned it sounds, bor-
rowed from another century. Yet today, even the
weather is bureaucratically gray. The buildings so
suddenly officious under all their flags. One hangs
listless from a window, more like laundry meant to
dry than majestic. Another tiny flag waves atop the
watertower's drab cabana.

In the background is the sound of hammering
and all around, the feel of those larger-than-life
striding above the city, busy. Then, just before I
came in, a small mustache of light appeared like
the aphorism of a quick kiss.

⁜

Tarpaper
beaded
with water.

A centipede
crosses a line.
The sun
crosses a line too.

Went higher up this morning
onto a ledge I hadn't noticed
and found the Yellow Pages
open to "T"

Taj Mahal
Talent Partners
Talk To The Hand Inc.
Tangerine Café
Target Trading
Tattoo Photography
Tell It To A Star

Wonder who they were trying to call?
Wonder who *they* is?

Chilly wind keeps slamming the door open
like a ghost. Keeps turning the pages
of my notebook. Rereading: "Mornings

are so dazzling. I hadn't noticed this
quality in them before." Yet now know
every pebble, powder-puff-plant, paint smudge

as if by name, whispered. One always aesthetically
pleasing moment is when a dove settles on the
forest-green trim of the Win Restaurant Supply Co.
across the street. Or when sun lights the bricks
of an adjacent building turning them a deep salmon.

✛

Cold Lookout

Sky
     a graveyard.

Ours is a city
of writing implements.

For nearly fifty years
I've been at war
with my body—

its explosive
women's ways.

When young
I always wanted to be
first a martyr—
then a spy.

One who moved
through fall colors
with a secret plan,

blank sheet of paper
carefully folded
in my pocket.

I like blending in
but should there be
someone watching
all they'd see is a hooded figure
on a rooftop.

Mala beads in gloved hands.
Lips moving.

I plant my syllables in light.
Let them multiply there.

How purposefully
everyone walks
the shadow-splashed streets
as if on their way
to a new job.

No loitering.

10/18/01 – 11/9/01

VARIATIONS ON THE HORIZON

In the morning he was Apollo or Ra—

the ancient one, but by noon he was just plain
Yahweh, and by evening, Sly, a nameless gust
who played the wind chimes increasing the
number of ants on the march, vociferous as all
get-out beneath their shag carpet of flame.
Miles turned the rotisserie until the book was
charred and black. Knowledge back then was
edible and served on the backs of broad green
leaves. The Kabbalists kept count of everything.
That were their way. Some wrote buildings and
tried to rewrite the stairway but the banister
broke off in my hand—soggy and splintered and
solipsistic. Still, I liked the way it continued like
a church picnic with no church to return to.
Perhaps I was flattered to think my presence
made some sort of contribution or that I was
touched by something improvisational yet all
worked out. Almost but not quite . . . almost
but not quite

the ever-elusive,
Mr. & Mrs. Spirit

SALA

messy room

cluttered
with old issues
of old issues

whose white walls
are never pristine
as white paper

the page
cannot hold
as well as a room

the body needs
a place to scrawl

its address
            shorthand

love
to return to
absentmindedly

NOTES

"Your Purple Arrives" is a line taken from Louis Zukofsky.

"The Sensuous Reader" and "Return of the Sensuous Reader" were inspired by the sexy, self-help classic *The Sensuous Woman* and its sequel—both by "J."

"Knock, Knock." Ganesha is a Hindu deity famous for removing obstacles. His image is often placed near the entrance of homes.

"The Movie Version" quotes an Emily Dickinson poem in its entirety. This piece also owes much in tone to Wayne Koestenbaum's poetry and writings on celebrity.

"A Cup of Joe" is for artist and poet Joe Brainard.

The August of "For August in April" refers not only to the eighth month of the year, but also to one of my favorite poets, August Kleinzahler.

"After and In Keeping With H.D." is a rewrite of an H.D. poem called "When I Am a Cup."

"Reset" was written as a response to a prescription for insomnia given me by a doctor who suggested that I sit in the sun, facing east, for one hour each morning in order to reset my inner clock. I chose the roof of my apartment building as the site for this ritual.

"Sala" is the Spanish word for room. It is also my husband Jerome's last name.

FUNDER ACKNOWLEDGMENT

Coffee House Press is an independent nonprofit literary publisher. Our books are made possible through the generous support of grants and gifts from many foundations, corporate giving programs, individuals, and through state and federal support. This project received major funding from the National Endowment for the Arts, a federal agency. Coffee House Press also received support from the Minnesota State Arts Board, through an appropriation by the Minnesota State Legislature; and from grants from the Elmer and Eleanor Andersen Foundation; the Beim Foundation; Buuck Family Foundation; the Bush Foundation; the Butler Family Foundation; Lerner Family Foundation; the McKnight Foundation; the law firm of Schwegman, Lundberg, Woessner & Kluth, P.A.; St. Paul Companies; Target, Marshall Field's, and Mervyn's with support from the Target Foundation; James R. Thorpe Foundation; The Walker Foundation; Wells Fargo Foundation Minnesota; West Group; the Woessner Freeman Foundation; and many individual donors.

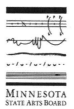 *This activity is made possible in part by a grant from the Minnesota State Arts Board, through an appropriation by the Minnesota State Legislature and a grant from the National Endowment for the Arts.* MINNESOTA STATE ARTS BOARD

 NATIONAL ENDOWMENT FOR THE ARTS

To you and our many readers across the country,
we send our thanks for your continuing support.